T0355019

FROZEN FLAME

FROZEN FLAME

ZAHRA NANJI

Archway Publishing books may be ordered through booksellers or by contacting:

Archway Publishing
1663 Liberty Drive
Bloomington, IN 47403
www.archwaypublishing.com
844-669-3957

ISBN: 978-1-6657-7215-0 (sc)
ISBN: 978-1-6657-7227-3 (hc)
ISBN: 978-1-6657-7216-7 (e)

Library of Congress Control Number: 2025901499

Print information available on the last page.

Archway Publishing rev. date: 01/25/2025

CONTENTS

Flicker to Flame

Part 3 Flame

EMBRACING THE FLAWS

Each petal unfurling, a story to tell,
Of trials and triumphs, of rising and fell.
Through storms that once battered, through shadows of doubt,
A peace blooms within as we learn to stand out.
So here in this moment, let us stand still,
In the embrace of acceptance, our spirits can fill.
For growth is a journey, a sacred release,
Where the heart finds its rhythm, where we gather our peace.

PART ONE
FROST

REJECTION

In the terrain of rejection, I tread with weary feet,
A dance of unrequited hopes, where pain and longing meet.
I'm asked to fight this bitter foe, to armor up and cope,
But how can I, when the one who rejects me is the same who
claims to love and hope?

Get used to rejection, they say, as if it's a friend to embrace,
But the weight of these dismissals leaves a hollow, empty space.
For in the depths of my yearning heart, I seek solace and desire,
Yet the one who rejects me forgets they once stoked this passionate
fire.

They ask me to fight the plague, to rise above the conflict,
But how can I battle rejection, when they once held me in sweetest
life?
Their love, once a sweet melody, played upon my eager soul,
Now reduced to whispers, fading echoes, a love that takes its toll.

Pleasure was once shared, like a delicate, secret dance,
But now it's a distant memory, a fleeting, stolen chance.
How can I get used to rejection, when the one who turns me
away,
Is the same who once loved me, craved me, made my heart sway?

I yearn to understand, to unravel this perplexing maze,
To find solace in the depths of rejection's haunting haze.
But the truth remains elusive, slipping through my grasp like sand,
As I try to comprehend how love and rejection intertwine, hand
in hand.

So I'll keep walking this path, though it's full of pain and despair,
Hoping that someday, rejection's burden - I'll no longer bear.
For in the delicate creation of love and its reverberations,
I'll find the strength to rise above, to set my spirit free.

And though rejection may linger, its sting less harsh and severe,
I'll remember the love that once was, the moments we held dear.
No longer burdened by their rejection, I'll find peace within my
soul,
For I am more than just a vessel, deserving of love that makes
me whole.

VESSEL OF SCARS

I am a broken piece of shit you are trying to heal,
A vessel of scars and wounds, too damaged to conceal.
But your energy, like gentle waves upon the shore,
Calming, soothing, whispering, "You're worth so much more."

Yet I, an addict to pain, find solace in despair,
A twisted romance with darkness, the weight I cannot bear.
Love me, my dear, so fiercely that I forget
The depths of my sorrow, the memories I regret.

Wrap your arms around me, hold me tight,
Let your love be the light that guides me through the night.
For in your embrace, a safe home I find,
A break from the chaos that haunts my troubled mind.

Your touch, a balm that soothes my shattered soul,
Your words, like music, mending what has been torn whole.
But still, I crave and run from the echoes of anguish within,
For pain has become my closest kin.

Love me, my dear, until I no longer ache,
Until the scars upon my heart begin to fade.
Whisper to me, in tender tones, of hope and light,
Help me forget the darkness that consumes me every night.

But know, my love, that I am a broken piece,
A mosaic of shattered dreams, longing for release.
Love me, even in my and for brokenness, for I yearn,
To finally learn what it means to truly return.

To return to a place where sorrows are lost,
Where love reigns supreme, and pain bears no cost.
Heal me, my dear, with your unwavering love,
And I promise, together, we'll rise above.

For I am the broken, the damaged, the lost,
Yet with you by my side, I'll pay any cost.
Love me, my dear, until I'm whole once more,
And with your love, I'll forget what sorrows are.

BROKEN FRAGMENTS

In the depths of my longing, I wait,
For life to be fair and happy, a gentle embrace.
But alas, it has different plans for me,
A cruel twist of fate, a relentless decree.

It throws me pain, like shards of glass,
Suffering, a relentless storm that does not pass.
Hurt, a constant companion by my side,
Bliss, a fleeting dream, elusive as the tide.

Torture, it whispers in my ear,
Heartbreak, a dagger that cuts deep and clear.
Failure, a bitter taste upon my tongue,
At every given moment, when hope should have sprung.

I yearn for solace, a reprieve from this conflict,
But life, in its wisdom, leads me on a different path.
Through these trials, I find strength in my core,
A resilience that blooms, as I weather the storm.

For in the darkest moments, I learn to rise,
To navigate the shadows with unyielding eyes.
And though life may not be fair or kind,
I gather fragments of resilience, piece by piece, in my mind.

I am a warrior, forged in the fire of pain,
From broken fragments, I build my domain.
And in the face of adversity, I shall remain,
A witness to the human spirit's unyielding flame.

So I wait, not for life to be fair or happy,
But for the strength to endure, to overcome the chaos.
For even in the face of life's relentless test,
I shall rise above, and find my peace and rest.

WORTHLESS

Don't love me, for I am not worth
A heart so fragile, a soul torn apart.
I am but a vessel of broken dreams,
A tapestry of flaws, stitched with despair.

In this vast expanse of life's grand stage,
I am but a whisper, lost in the wind's embrace.
My worth is but a fleeting shadow,
Cast upon the canvas of forgotten souls.

Do not hold me close, for I am numb,
A barren land where love cannot bloom.
I am the remnants of shattered hopes,
Drowning in the ocean of my own self-doubt.

I am the jagged edges of a broken mirror,
Reflecting a distorted image of who I was.
Don't love me, for I am not worthy,
Of the warmth and tenderness that love bestows.

My heart is a cavern, dark and cold,
Echoing with the scars of battles untold.
I am but a poem, inked with melancholy,
Written in the language of sorrow and regret.

Don't love me, for I am a tempest's rage,
A hurricane that leaves destruction in its wake.
I am the thunder's roar, the lightning's strike,
A force that brings chaos and turmoil.

But if you choose to love me still,
Know that I am a canvas waiting to be filled.
For beneath the layers of doubt and despair,
There lies a glimmer of hope, waiting to be shared.

Love me not for what I am or what I've been,
But for the potential that lies within.
For even in darkness, there is a flicker of light,
A chance for redemption, a reason to fight.

So, don't love me, I am not worth,
But if you choose to, see beyond my dearth.
Hold my hand, and together we shall find,
A love that transcends the boundaries of time.

For in the vast expanse of this universe,
Love has the power to heal and immerse.
And though I may not be worthy in my own eyes,
With your love, I can learn to rise.

SELFISH SOUL

Let me paint a portrait of a selfish soul,
A being consumed by desires untamed and bold.
Behold, the pure and perfect definition of me,
A creature longing for love, craving endlessly,
With no regard for the hearts left shattered,
Or the time stolen, as if it never mattered.

I, the master of self-indulgence, stand tall,
With a hunger insatiable, devouring all,
For I am the thief of affections and care,
Taking from you, leaving nothing but despair.

In this grand convention of life and emotion,
I weave deceit and manipulation with devotion,
For my desires are paramount, my needs supreme,
The world revolves around me, or so it would seem.

But let us delve deeper into this grand facade,
Unmask the motivations, strip away the charade,
Beneath the layers of selfishness, do you not see,
A fragile soul, yearning to be set free?

For in this quest for love, I too am lost,
A victim of my own desires and torment, at great cost,
The more I take, the emptier I become,
A void within, where compassion should hum.

So, I implore you, dear, to understand,
That this selfish me, a flawed creation, I am,
The path of selflessness, I strive to attain,
To break free from this cycle, to ease the pain.

For love is not a commodity to hoard,
Nor time a currency to be recklessly poured,
In this magnificent bond of life, we are all connected,
To deny this truth, we remain forever disconnected.

So, let us learn from the selfish me portrayed,
To cherish the love we receive, never betrayed,
And in the grand symphony of life, let us find,
A harmony that unites.

HOPELESS

In the depths of despair, I shall abide,
For I am but a wretched soul, denied.
Do not love me, seek not my heart's embrace,
For it is shrouded in darkness, devoid of grace.

Within these hollow bones, sorrow takes its hold,
A melody of misery, forever untold.
Do not love me, for my spirit is but dust,
Lost in the winds of time, reduced to rust.

Hold not my hand, for it is stained with ink,
Words of self-loathing, this heart will never shrink.
Do not love me, for I am as a broken dream,
A shattered mirror's gleam, reflecting esteem.

Yet, in this desolation, purpose may yet rise,
A flicker of hope amidst tear-stricken skies.
Do not love me, but instead, love my potential,
To bloom from despair, a flower so essential.

For though I may falter, stumble along the way,
These worthless ashes may yet find a brighter day.
Do not love me, but love the phoenix unseen,
Rising from this darkness, crowning glory shall convene.

So, heed my plea, dear soul, do not let love befall,
For I am but a hopeless canvas, craving its last call.
Do not love me, for there is nothing left to give,
But maybe, just maybe, in your heart, I'll live.

DEPTS OF SORROWS

In the depths of sorrow's grip, I find myself,
Life's cruel hand has shown me deep hurt,
A pain that lingers, an ache that clings,
And in this darkness, I yearn to disappear.

Like a whisper carried by the wind,
I wish to fade, to vanish in the evening shade,
For this world has grown heavy on my shoulders,
And I fear the weight will crush what is left of my soul.

No footsteps left behind no trace to be found,
I'll become a ghost, lost in the swarm of bees,
Where no one can follow, no one can reach,
A nomad of the heart, drifting in solitude's embrace.

Tempting it is to dissolve into nothingness,
To become a fleeting memory, a forgotten name,
But even in my darkest hour, a spark remains,
A tiny flame that refuses to be extinguished.

For within this pain, I find strength anew,
A resilience forged by the fires of despair,
And though life's wounds may scar and break,
I know, deep within, I am not meant to disappear.

So, I may rise from the ashes, like a phoenix reborn,
The echoes of hurt may linger, but I'll find my voice,
For I am more than the sum of my sorrow,
And my spirit, unyielding, a will that cannot be erased.

In the fight of existence, I have a place,
A purpose, a story yet to be told,
And though the road ahead may be treacherous,
I will navigate the shadows, undeterred and bold.

So, let the world search, let them seek,
But they shall find no trace of my surrender,
For I am here, invisible yet resilient,
And in this universe, I am meant to endure.

CAGED ANIMAL

I am a caged animal, that is living with everyone,
A restless spirit, yearning to break free,
Bound by the confines of a world that suffocates,
I seek liberation, from this cage of conformity.

In the depths of my being, a wild flame burns,
An untamed force, longing to roam,
I hear the distant call of the untrodden path,
Enticing me to escape these walls of stone.

With each passing day, my spirit grows weary,
Trapped in the monotony of a scripted life,
But deep within, a rebellion stirs,
A rebellion that craves the taste of the unknown.

I am a caged animal, trying to escape,
Trapped within the confines of a world unyielding,
My spirit yearns for freedom, for a taste of the wild,
Yet these iron bars confine my restless soul.

I pace the length of my imprisonment,
Each step a desperate plea for release,
My heart pounds against the unyielding cage,
Like thunder echoing through the empty air.

Oh, how I long to feel the wind upon my face,
To taste the sweetness of untamed freedom,
To run with the wild ones, unburdened and free,
But alas, these walls confine my wild heart.

I claw at the cage with untamed fury,
My nails scraping against the unyielding metal,
Each mark a demonstration to my unquenchable desire,
To break free from this prison that binds me.

But the bars remain unyielding, unbroken,
And I am left to ponder my fate,
Will I forever be a captive of this existence,
Or is there hope for this caged animal's escape?

I dream of open fields and starlit nights,
Of running through the forests, swift and strong,
Of surrendering to the call of the wilderness,
And embracing the freedom that has long eluded me.

But until that day arrives, I shall not surrender,
I shall not let this cage define my worth,
For within me, there burns a fire,
A flame that refuses to be extinguished.

So, I shall continue to fight, to strive,
To break these chains that bind me tight,
For I am a caged animal, longing to be free,
And my spirit shall soar, beyond these walls, one day

I AM FINE, WILL BE FINE

I am fine, will be fine, always have been,
A mantra whispered softly to my restless soul.
Through trials and tribulations, I have seen,
A steadfast spirit that refuses to fold.

In the darkest nights, when shadows loom,
I stand tall, unwavering in my resolve.
For within me burns a fire, a fierce flame,
Igniting hope that cannot be dissolved.

Through storms that rage and tear at my core,
I find solace in the depths of my being.
For I am not defined by the tempest's roar,
But by the strength that I am foreseeing.

I am a warrior, a fighter, unyielding,
With scars that tell tales of battles fought.
Each wound a reminder of the strength I'm wielding,
Witness to the resilience I've sought.

With every challenge faced, I grow stronger,
Embracing the struggle, not fearing its might.
For within me lies a power, a power that lingers,
A force that propels me through the darkest night.

I am fine, will be fine, always have been,
An unwavering spirit that refuses to break.
For life's trials are but a test, a scene,
And I am determined to rise and partake.

So, fear not for me, dear, I implore,
For I am fine, will be fine, always have been.
With every step forward, I grow more,
A test to the strength that lies within.

LONELINESS

In the depths of my soul, loneliness resides,
A constant companion, lurking, it abides.
It wraps itself around me, a shadowy shroud,
Leaving me gasping, silenced, no words allowed.

But within this darkness, a fire still burns,
A spirit unwavering, determined, it yearns.
To fight for connection, for love to ignite,
To banish the loneliness, reclaiming my light.

With each passing day, a battle ensues,
Between loneliness and the fight I must choose.
I stand tall, courageous, ready to defend,
My heart and my spirit, refusing to bend.

Loneliness may whisper, slither and deceive,
But my resilience rises, I will not grieve.
For deep within, a strength emerges, anew,
A powerful force, blazing skies vibrant and blue.

I gather my courage, embracing the fight,
To conquer the darkness, restore what is right.
For within this struggle, I find solace strong,
Knowing that I'm not alone, that I truly belong.

In the depths of my soul, I'll ignite a spark,
A flame that consumes, illuminates the dark.
Loneliness may linger, but I won't give in,
For the fight within me, love and hope shall win

DAMAGED SOUL

In the depths of my being, a damaged soul resides,
Both inside and out, scars etched deep within my hide.
For I am a vessel, once brimming with emotions untold,
Now empty, devoid of the feelings I once held.

I long to care, to love, to mend your shattered heart,
But in my brokenness, I tear your world apart.
The touch of my hand, once meant to comfort and heal,
Now leaves you wounded, unable to fully feel.

Within the walls of my heart, tears silently flow,
For failing to communicate, to let my love show.
Your pain, a mirror of the suffering I've endured,
And yet, my own wounds remain unassured.

I yearn to be your solace, to help you find release,
Though I know I may never find my own inner peace.
A damaged soul, forever burdened by its plight,
Lost in the darkness, devoid of joy and delight.

But still, I strive to help you heal, to bring you light,
Even if my own redemption stays forever out of sight.
For in the depths of my damaged soul, a glimmer remains,
A flicker of hope, amidst the sea of my own pains.

So let me be your guide, through the shadows we tread,
Together we'll navigate the darkness, hand in hand.
For though I am a damaged soul, with no return to bliss,
I'll walk this path with you and promise not to miss.
Any chance for you to heal under my damaged soul

TOO DAMAGED

I am a damaged soul, in and out,
a vessel worn by pain and doubt.
No longer do I feel, no longer do I cry,
emptiness now resides behind my weary eyes.

I hurt you when I want to care,
a twisted dance of love and despair.
My touch, once warm, now cold as ice,
leaving scars upon your fragile paradise.

Within, I weep for the words unsaid,
failing to reach you, leaving you misled.
Your pain, a mirror of my own,
a haunting reminder of how I've grown.

I yearn to heal you, to mend your wounded heart,
but how can I offer solace when I'm falling apart?
For I am a damaged soul, forever scarred,
trapped in a cycle that cannot be unbarred.

Happiness eludes me, as pleasure fades away,
like a fleeting dream, it dissipates, they say.
Feelings, once vibrant, now muted and numb,
a symphony of sorrow, where once joy had strummed.

So I shall linger in this realm of broken dreams,
in the shadows where hope's light barely gleams.
I may never be healed, but if I can help you find
a glimmer of solace, it'll be worth every decline.

For I am a damaged soul, a person lost at sea,
but even in my brokenness, I'll strive to set you free.

NO PEACE WITHIN

I scramble for attention, no peace within me,
A soul caught in the vortex of uncertainty,
I struggle with attachments, their weight upon my chest,
As I fumble through the labyrinth, unable to rest.

How do I resonate, how do I converse,
With the ones I hold dear, in this cosmic curse.
Words fall like raindrops, scattered and lost,
Their meaning diluted, their essence exhaust.

In this ecosystem, I am but a speck,
Lost in a universe that I cannot connect.
My thoughts wander, searching for a bridge,
To span the divide and release this inner siege.

I yearn for connection, a bond that holds tight,
But my heart is a puzzle, locked in endless night.
I stumble through conversations, my words incomplete,
As fear and doubt dance, an intricate deceit.

I long to be understood, to be seen and heard,
Yet my voice falters, like a wounded bird.
I am adrift, in a sea of untold emotions,
Yearning for support, for soothing devotion.

Oh, how I crave the tranquility of unity,
To be embraced in love's warm serenity.
But I, a wanderer, lost in my own maze,
Struggle to find the path that leads to love's embrace.

So I scramble for attention, with restless heart,
Hoping to find solace, to make a fresh start.
In this wilderness of longing, I seek to find,
The key to unlock the chambers of my mind.

But until then, I am a soul in disarray,
Seeking peace within, in my own unique way.
I'll continue to wander, stumble and fall,
Hoping that one day, love will conquer all.

CHOICE I MADE

I made a choice, and we suffered,
Bound by fate's firm hand.
No apology can make up for my choices,
For in this darkness we now stand.

Destiny's humble twist brought us together,
Entangled in a web we cannot sever.
The weight of my decisions upon us pressed,
As we bear the burden, happy and seasoned.

No words can undo the pain I've caused,
No comfort found in apologies tossed.
I see the despair etched upon your face,
As we endure the consequences, our hearts encased.

In this long and endless night,
We walk hand in hand, shadowed by dilemma.
The echoes of regret echo through,
A constant reminder of the damage we accrue.

But amidst this chaos, a flicker of hope,
A glimmer of light in this desolate scope.
For in our shared suffering, we find strength,
We endure the brunt, no matter the length.

Our affection, tested by the trials we face,
Blossoms in adversity, defying its grace.
Together we weather the storms that arise,
Bound by the choices, yet our love still flies.

And though the road is treacherous and long,
We'll face the consequences, brave and strong.
For in this journey, we learn to forgive,
To find redemption and the will to live and heal.

So let us embrace the scars we bear,
In this twisted tale, where pain is our share.
For within the darkness, a new dawn will break,
And our choices redeemed, a brighter path we'll make.

LEAVE YOU

I never meant to blow you off,
To leave you standing in the cold,
With hollow words and promises,
I never meant to hurt you so.

Time slipped through my careless grasp,
As priorities tangled and clashed,
But in my heart, you remained,
A flickering flame, forever unexplained

Regret now fills my weary soul,
For the pain I caused, the toll I took,
I wish I could rewind, make it whole,
But the past is etched, an open book.

So here I stand, with humble plea,
Begging for forgiveness, can't you see?
I never meant to blow you off,
To leave you wondering, feeling lost.

Let me mend what's been torn apart,
With whispered apologies from my heart,
For I never meant to hurt you so,
I never meant to let you go.

WON'T SHARE WITH ME

You won't share with me, a sting to my soul,
A heavy cloak of disappointment draped upon my heart.
For in this vast sea of belonging,
Why do you withhold, keeping us apart?

The world abounds with treasures untold,
Riches of laughter, love, and joy to be shared.
Yet you stand firm, your heart icy and cold,
Denying me the warmth and tenderness I've dared.

In the realm of friendship's embrace,
Where secrets are traded like sacred tales,
I stand on the outskirts, a dejected face,
Yearning for the connection that forever prevails.

What have I done to deserve this fate?
To be cast aside, an outcast of your trust.
I've bared my soul, opened the gates,
Yet you remain steadfast, unyielding, unjust.

Is it fear that grips your heart so tight,
To expose your vulnerabilities, your innermost desires?
Or is it selfishness, a need to hold all might,
To hoard the treasures that friendship inspires?

But I beseech you, let down your walls,
Allow my presence to seep into your core.
For in sharing, true friendship enthralls,
And a bond so strong, we've never known before.

In the vast expanse of life's grand design,
We are but fleeting moments, destined to fade.
So don't let pride and selfishness define,
The legacy of regret that we have made.

Open your heart, dear friend, and see,
The beauty that lies in sharing and trust.
For in unity, we find serenity,
And friendship's flame burns bright, it truly must.

So let us cast away the chains of restraint,
Embrace the freedom that sharing brings.
For in this dance of souls, we'll find no taint,
Only the melody of friendship, soaring on love's wings.

You won't share with me, but I won't despair,
For I know the power of generosity's decree.
And in the end, my friend, I'll always be there,
Ready to share my love, unconditionally.

FROST TO FLICKER

WHISPERS OF HOPE

In the shadow's embrace,
whispers of the night Stars flicker like distant memories,
cold and still,
Emptiness echoes where dreams once held a thrill,
A veil of silence cloaks all in its might.

From this abyss,
dawn teases with a gentle sway,
Light cracks open the horizon's tightened seam,
Hope blooms where despair reigned supreme,
Yet darkness lingers,
refusing to fully decay.

PART TWO

FLICKER

PART TWO

FLICKER

A TALE TO TELL

In the depths of my soul, I dwell
With pain indescribable, a tale to tell
For within me resides a hurt profound
Given by a loved one, a heart unwound

Oh, the consequences of broken trust
Like shards of glass, they pierce, they thrust
Leaving scars upon my vulnerable heart
A tribute to love torn apart

I bear the weight of shattered dreams
In the refuge of shadows, I now convene
Fearful of loving and trusting with such depth again
As the wounds within me slowly mend

In this domain of sorrow and despair
I navigate through the darkness, stripped bare
Yet, amidst the ache and relentless strife
I find solace in the fragments of my life

For in pain, sometimes, freedom is born
A chance to rise, to be reborn
To forge my own path, untethered, unbound
With resilience as my armor, firmly crowned

I embrace the bittersweet dance of fate
Navigating the realms of love and hate
With every step, I grow stronger, wiser too
Leaving behind what no longer serves, what no longer rings true

I live with pain indescribable, it's true
But it does not define me, this I pursue
For within these scars lies a story untold
Of a spirit that rises, unyielding and bold

So let the pain be the ink that paints my verse
My soul shall immerse
For in the stretch of my poetic art
I find healing, redemption, and a brand-new start

SEPARATED PASSION

In the domain where words fall short,
And love transcends the confines of speech,
I stand, humbled, unable to convey
The depths of my affection for you.

No sonnet or verse, no rhyme or prose,
Can encapsulate the magnitude of this love,
For it blooms beyond the world of language,
In a universe where souls merge.

No kiss, though passionate and intense,
Can capture the fire that burns within,
No touch, however gentle and tender,
Can match the intimacy we share.

Two bodies, vessels of desire and longing,
Yet bound by a connection deeper than flesh,
We are but vessels, pure conduits of energy,
Two souls connected, united in purpose.

Separated by the distance,
Yet connected by a thread invisible,
Our hearts beat in perfect synchrony,
A rhythm only we can comprehend.

We defy the boundaries of the tangible,
Our love knows no limits, no boundaries,
We dance in the orbit of the intangible,
Where words cease and spirits soar.

No words, no kiss, no touch can suffice,
To describe the love that binds us so,
For we are two bodies, one soul,
An exquisite union, a love untamed.

And so, I stand in awe and wonder,
At the beauty of this love we share,
With no words to describe its essence,
I surrender, and let our souls speak.

MY SECRET

Oh, don't let the smile cheat you
turmoil in my heart like a wave of tsunami
feelings, that, make me helpless everyday
stand next to me, be my shoulder,
I shout, I scream, be my shoulder, understand me,
Listen! See! Feel! Hear!
I need you.

As a free bird once I was now captured,
Wings cut, Freedom captured
helpless, lifeless, suffocated
with no one next to me.
A voice within calls out to me
Be strong you can make it
You will be free
You will fly again
You will see the blue sky beneath you again

A plea from heart
but tears roll out
Can time be the way it was?
Can time be better than it is?
Or can time be what people trust it to be?
Better?
Worse?
I have lived to answer it.
I believed in it. I trusted it.
It broke me. It betrayed me.
Over and over again.
My heart bled; tears dried.
Only remembering what I got
Rejection.
Not from one but from all.

I remember my wholesome days
Have I done anything wrong?
Is anything my mistake?
Whatever that is happening is it something I am to blame?
Anyone? Someone? Help me answer it?
No? ... ... Yes ... ? Maybe... ...
Bring relief to what I feel, to what I think
To what my eyes see and show
Don't go with what you see
Understand me and show me
What is it that I did?
Is it me?
Am I to blame?
Did I do something?
Why is anything not enough?
Anything I touch withers,
Everything I say matters
You laugh but I am no joker,
Sometimes, somethings are better left concealed.

SHARE
I heard you say
as I open my mouth you ask me to listen
listen you say
sealing my mouth
my shoulder.
the momentum lost.

I hear you scream
SHARE
trusting you I open my mouth
uttering my fears, you look lost
lost in your thoughts far away from me

silent or laughing, did it make a difference?
Or was it just a story for you?
I ask myself.
Do you really care? Crushed.
Rejected by you in every way.
I stop trying. Giving up.
You seek my support.
Who do I rely on?

Once illustrious, cheerful
ecstatic for what it was
Share... A word now meaningless, deceitful
broken, unworthy for what it has
fabricated me in today

A helpful shoulder for others,
An ear to the broken,
This has been my life for as long as I remember,
You to open a forbidden door,
I am scared,
What if?
I just met you but it seems like I know you,
It is the first time someone really cared to ask,
Why is it I listen, and not talk,
Why not SHARE?

Excited I am. I don't know how to start.
It has been years since I said something and
Someone really paid attention
Someone really remembered,
That, I have feelings, I am a human,
Horrified with past experiences,

I sit silently, watching the waves,
How I wish all of this was true,
The scorching heat and warm winds
With someone I could spill my heart open to.

Watching the stars through my window, I smile,
Reliving the moment I met Jenny,
What a terrified scene it was,
The day we became friends.
Walking to the beach instead of college,
Sitting and recalling of what we had just encountered,
Time flied, and all I could see were her light brown eyes,
Honey coloured curly hair and that smile.
Still shaking. At first I thought it was from the long walk,
And our plan from skipping the class today,
But then I realized as we sat, now, relaxed with sea breeze
It was shock. We had just been robbed,
Knives on our throats. I realized I was shaking too.
I simpered as I recalled that day.

As days passed by, I realized the beauty was right with me
Unknown and unnoticed. Her simplicity, patience and voice
Appealing, attracting me towards her. Days passed we talked,
Days turned into weeks and weeks into months,
I heard everything she had to say. She was caring different than others,
Always thought of me. Counted me in. I existed for her,
For once I felt, that someone was there to listen and be with me.
I finally did not feel the need to write everything down.
But, I still did. My companion, my journals.

Today I will tell you - MY SECRET

GRAND STAGE OF EXISTENCE

I wait for life to be fair and happy,
But it has different plans for me, I see.
It throws me pain, suffering, hurt,
Respite, torture, heartbreak, and failure,
At every given moment possible.

In this grand stage of existence,
I stand as a mere pawn in its game.
Life, the master of unpredictability,
Unfolds its script with relentless fury,
Testing my strength, my resilience.

I yearn for fairness, for joy to prevail,
But life, it laughs at my naive desires.
I am but a vessel, tossed in its tempest,
A recipient of its whims and caprice,
Bound to endure its relentless hand.

Oh, the agony, the trials that befall,
Like a storm, they crash upon my soul.
Each blow, a fierce gust, a torrential rain,
Leaving scars etched deep within my being,
Reminding me of life's cruel refrain.

Yet, amidst the chaos, there lies respite,
A brief interlude where peace finds solace.
A fleeting moment, a balm for the wounds,
A glimpse of hope, a fragile oasis,
Before the next chapter of torment unfolds.

Life taunts me with its twisted dance,
A symphony of heartache and despair.
But in this symphony, there lies beauty,
A melancholic melody, a bitter sweetness,
That echoes through the chambers of my heart.

For it is through pain that I discover strength,
Through suffering that I find my resilience.
Life's relentless trials forge my spirit,
Shaping me into a warrior, unyielding,
For I refuse to succumb to its whims.

So let life throw its arsenal my way,
I will stand tall, unbowed by its blows.
For in the depths of my soul, I know,
That though life may be unfair and harsh,
I possess the courage to face its storms.

And though I long for fairness and happiness,
I understand that life's plans are not mine.
I embrace the journey, the twists and turns,
Knowing that within the chaos lies growth,
And that, my dear, is the essence of life.

CHAOS

I am apologetic as I know my relocation
Has uproared trauma from the past,
Tangled memories that haunt our hearts,
Leaving scars that refuse to heal.

I have lived in chaos, my presence
Causing our love, energies, and connection
To teeter on the edge of despair,
Tangled and strained, caught in the storm.

I beg for forgiveness, as time and distance
Have become a colossal barrier between us,
Stretching our souls thin, straining our bond,
Leaving us lost in the abyss of longing.

I am regretful, oh how I regret,
For bringing chaos to our once harmonious flow,
Disrupting the delicate course of our connection,
Leaving us tangled in a web of uncertainty.

But fear not, my love, for I am determined,
To fight the darkness that engulfs me,
To claw my way back into your embrace,
To rebuild what has been shattered.

I will not let the shadows consume me,
I will not let the chaos define our fate,
For I am adamant in my quest for peace,
To mend what has been broken by my hands.

So bear with me, my dearest,
As I navigate through this storm,
Know that my love for you remains unwavering,
And I will fight, relentlessly, to be better.

In the depths of my soul, a fire burns bright,
Guiding me towards a path of healing,
I vow to untangle the knots of my past,
And build a future illuminated by light.

Forgive me, my love, for the pain I've caused,
For the distance that divides us,
I promise to tread lightly on your fragile heart,
And together, with your guidance,
We shall conquer the chaos and be in light and flow.

HOW DO I PRAISE YOU

How do I praise you, my home, my love,
With music or with words, I ask?
For you are the essence of my being,
The sanctuary where my soul basks.

Shall I let the melodies of a thousand strings
Dance upon the air, in sweet harmony?
Or shall I paint a portrait with words,
To capture the essence of your beauty?

Oh, how the music would soar and swell,
A symphony of love and adoration,
Each note a testament to your grace,
A celebration of our sacred connection.

But words, oh words, how they too can weave
A tapestry of emotions, deep and true,
An intricately crafted declaration,
Of the love that binds me, only to you.

For you are the shelter that shields me,
From the storms that rage beyond our door,
The hearth that warms my weary heart,
When life's harsh winds make me sore.

Your embrace, my love, is like no other,
A haven where my dreams take flight,
And in your presence, I find peace,
As darkness surrenders to your gentle light.

How do I praise you, my love?
For you are more than the sum of your parts,
More than the beauty that meets the eye,
You are a sanctuary for the weary soul.

You cradle memories and dreams,
Nurture the seeds of hope and desire,
In your embrace, I find refuge,
A sanctuary from life's raging fire.

You are the canvas on which life is painted,
A tapestry of colors, woven with care,
And as I stand in awe of your grandeur,
I am humbled by the love you we share.

So how do I praise you, my love?
In words, I stumble and fall short,
For your essence defies description,
And your majesty transcends all bounds.

In music or in words, my love,
You are the muse that inspires my pen,
And forevermore, I shall sing your praises,
For you are my home, my love, again and again.

For in the quiet stillness of our togetherness,
Where love's symphony softly plays,
I offer my heart's sincerest gratitude,
To the home that has filled my restless days.

I FOUND A HOME

In fields of green, where wildflowers sway,
I met a friend, on a sunny day.
Her laughter bright and smile so wide,
I knew right then; she'd be my mine.

Her eyes, like stars, shone bright and clear,
Her voice, a melody, so pure and near.
We talked of dreams, and hopes, and fears,
And I knew, our bond would bring us tears.

We shared our stories, and our lives,
And found in each other, endless strife.
Through joy and pain, we'd stand as one,
And in each other, find our sun.

In her, I found a home, a place to be,
A love so strong, it set me free.
She's the one I turn to, in the night,
The one who makes my heart take flight.

So here's to you, my dearest friend,
The one who's always there, until the end.
In you, I've found a love so true,
A friendship that's forever, pure and through.

KINSHIP

In shadows cast by life's uncertain course,
A beautiful, strange friend emerged, divine,
A soul so rare, a spirit that could shine,
A bond so strong, a connection, no force.

With every word, a universe unfolded,
A melody of thoughts, a symphony,
In depths of laughter, tears, and reverie,
Our hearts entwined, a tapestry, unfolded.

Within your eyes, a world of wonder gleamed,
A kaleidoscope of dreams, untamed, free,
A mirror to my soul, reflecting me,
A friendship true, where love and light redeemed.
Through midnight conversations, we discovered,
A kinship that defied every boundary,
Our souls entwined, like lovers rediscovered,
A friendship that transcended all normalcy.

Oh, beautiful strange friend who became mine,
You have forever imprinted upon my soul,
A connection so rare, so divinely divine,
A tapestry of friendship, forever whole

A spirit, a beacon in times of despair,
A reminder that we're not alone in this journey,
With her by my side, I need not beware,
For we are bound, forever intertwined, eternally.

In this vast universe, filled with wonders untold,
I am grateful for the gift you've bestowed,
A friendship, unbreakable, steadfast and bold,
A bond, irreplaceable, forever to hold.

MEMORIES

I have lost my voice,
MYSELF. I am not me.
This is the new me.
Angry, Selfish, Hollow,
You left me wounded, bare, lost.
I see you today, like me,
Forgive me. I blame myself.

You are the light to my darkness,
Sweetness to my life,
Freshness to the tired soul.
You. I. We, I miss it.

The sight of you brings me memories,
Memories of us. Me. You.
Our first meet, me into you,
Your graceful gaze, charming eyes,
Those luscious moving lips,
Me lost staring in your eyes.
Deaf to your words,
Admiring your beauty.
Again. Today.
I am mesmerized after years.
Lost. Time; frozen at stand still.
Breathtaking, once more.
World moves but I am living in the past.
I try to find you, me and us.

Present holds a different set of cards,
You, with new folk.
Lost I am acquainted to old and new friends and foes,
Enemies all around. Wounds old and new,

Seasons turned new leaves,
Giving us different chances,
Reminder of all the vices.
Karma as you mentioned.

I realize how lonely I am,
Surrounded in a crowd of fault and fraud.
I live life of showbiz and masquerade,
Pleasing and entertainment,
None that is me.
Craving rebirth after rebirth,
I morphed myself in cloths of silk,
All I need is you.
Not silk.
It is love.
Arms of warmth,
Sense of belonging,
Gentle caress,
Air of home,
Scent of calmness,
Soothing noises and screams,
And, a garden full of life,
With you. US. We.

That was me.
What about you? I see you.
A childlike smile on the face,
Hiding sorrows no-one can tell.
Oh dear!
My love, what has time done to us.
Why are you so far from me and so near to me?
I hear your heartbeat in me. Alive. As you in me.
We are one soul then why apart.

I failed you. I didn't listen to you.
We both cried out the same.
I maintain my love for you,
Same. Fierce, Obsessive, Possessive
Gentle, Protective and ever-living.
Today, I declare.
I want, I need you back in my life.
I make all the amends. I ask you to be mine.
Will you? Do you? Are you still mine?

I want to return the energy,
Enthusiasm in your smile,
The courage, the life, the strength,
Willingness, purity and love.
I am selfish. I want to help
For me. Not for you, so I can find the home
I have lost with you.

I want to create the home we both cared for,
We both dream for. Together. You and me.
Tell me. Do I still see you right?

What has the world done to you?
You are loosing your spark,
Shine in your eyes,
Fake laughter and a pasted smile,
Overdressed like a doll with clothes you hate,
I want to know more.
What are you hiding?
What is in this heart of yours?
What has the world done?
Why is it you fear to stretch you hand to me?

I am standing in-front of you,
Hand forward - you hesitant.
Heartbroken. I am waiting.

We are meant to be together,
See it. Feel it.
Our paths cross over and over,
You refused. I agreed. Now I insist on staying.
I want and need my home.
I can't see you endure any misery,
I am staying.

Hate me. Love me.
I am here. More stubborn than before
With more love than before.
Am done listening to you,
Baring the fruit of abiding to you,
Result. Both of us crushed; unhappy.
Hold my hand. Accept me. Accept us.
Let us make our home. I, Me, You and Us.
Our path is meant to be one.
Don't deny it. Don't fight it.

You are mine. I am yours.
Let us make this ours.
A life where we move forward,
Careless, carefree, no bounds, no rules.

We smile and cry
Every time. No matter the occasion.
We explore and create an adventure.
Everyday. Together. You and Me. US. We.

Grab my hand. Let us do it.
Let us make this world ours.
Let's make this an adventure of life.

Broken apart - together we are strong unbreakable
soul,
Home strong than ever.

INTERTWINED

In this vast expanse of time and space,
Where distance stretches like an endless chase,
We find ourselves entwined, yet worlds apart,
A paradox of love, a fragile work of art.

For when we stand side by side, so near,
Beneath the same sky, our souls so clear,
It's hard to be apart, to breathe apart,
When you're right here, within my heart.

I see you, I feel you, and I long to be,
Closer still, where our souls are set free,
But fate has dealt its hand, a cruel decree,
Keeping us apart, bound by destiny.

Oh, the agony of not being near,
When your presence fills my every fear,
It's difficult to resist the urge, the desire,
To hold you close, to set our hearts on fire.

Your eyes, like stars, they captivate,
Drawing me closer, tempting my fate,
And yet, I must resist, for we are apart,
Though you stand right here, igniting my heart.

The ache within, it grows with each passing day,
As I yearn for your touch, for your love to stay,
But in this moment, in this fragile dance,
We find solace in knowing, in this circumstance.

For even though we can't embrace, can't share,
The love we hold, so strong, so rare,
We cherish the moments, the stolen glances,
And find solace in the power of our romances.

So, let us endure this test of time,
Knowing our love transcends any rhyme,
For though it's hard to be apart, my dear,
Our souls are forever, eternally near.

MAGNETIC PULL

Magnetic pull, your connection,
A force that defies all comprehension,
No rhyme nor reason can explain,
The bond between us, an eternal flame.

Like two opposite poles, we attract,
Drawn together, there's no turning back,
The universe conspires, aligning stars,
As we dance in sync, no matter how far.

Your presence, a magnetic field,
Pulling me close, making me yield,
To the power of our cosmic embrace,
In this vast world, we've found our place.

No boundaries can hold us apart,
For our connection is a work of art,
Unrestrained, it flows and expands,
A magnetic force we can't reprimand.

Through the chaos and the noise,
We find solace in each other's voice,
An invisible thread that binds our souls,
A connection that surpasses all controls.

Like magnets, we navigate the unknown,
Guided by a force not easily shown,
In this vast universe, we have found,
A love that's boundless and knows no ground.

So let us revel in this magnetic pull,
Embrace the connection that makes us whole,
For in this dance of attraction, we find,
A love that transcends space and time.

GUIDE ME

My words don't align with my actions
But my love, oh my love for you
It fills this heart to the brim
With a warmth that never fades
It lingers in every beat, every breath

I may stumble and falter
In my attempts to show you
Just how much you mean to me
But please believe, my darling
My love for you is pure and true

I may not always say the right words
Or do the right things
But know this, my love
My heart is yours, completely
And it beats for you, always

I may not be the perfect partner
I may disappoint and fail
But in every mistake I make
There is a love that never wavers
A love that stands strong, unwavering

So forgive me, my love
For my shortcomings and faults
And know that in every misstep
There is a heart that loves you
A heart that is yours, forever true

My words may not always align with my actions
But my love for you will never falter
It will always burn bright
Guiding me back to you
For you are my love, my everything.

WITH YOU I HEAL

With you I heal and I am me,
In your presence, my soul is set free.
Like a river, flowing and untamed,
You ignite a fire that can't be tamed.

In your arms, I find solace and peace,
A sanctuary where my worries cease.
You mend the wounds that life has dealt,
And in your love, my heart is felt.

With you, I'm no longer bound by chains,
No longer haunted by past pains.
You see through the layers that others can't,
Uncover the beauty, reveal the enchant.

In your eyes, I see acceptance and grace,
A reflection of love that I embrace.
You hold my hand, guiding me through,
Together we conquer, old and new.

With you, I find strength to face the storm,
To weather the battles, to transform.
You're my shelter, my anchor, my rock,
In your embrace, I find the key to unlock.

With you, I discover my truest form,
A love that's pure, a love that's warm.
With each passing day, we grow and learn,
Through the twists and turns, we discern.

With you, I heal and I am me,
In your love, I find my harmony.
Forever grateful, I'll hold you near,
For with you, my love, I have no fear.

YEARNING

Finally we met after days of yearning,
Lovers can't be apart, love is growing,
And getting insatiable, an eternal flame burning,
In this universe, our souls linked.

Days stretched on like an eternity,
Each passing moment an ache in my chest,
Longing for your touch, your presence,
Yearning for the connection we both confessed.

Our hearts, like magnets, drawn together,
Across the distance, our love did soar,
Through endless nights, under starlit skies,
We knew in our souls, we couldn't ignore.

The anticipation, the desire, palpable,
As we counted down the hours and minutes,
Each second a witness to our love and devotion,
The longing building, passion reaching its limits.

And then, at last, our worlds collided,
In that moment, time stood still,
Our embrace, a harbour of love,
As our souls danced, a cosmic thrill.

The hunger within us, insatiable,
Fuelling the fire that consumes our beings,
We surrender, bodies entwined,
In this love, we find our truest meanings.

No words can capture the depth of our connection,
No bounds can contain the love we share,
In this world, we're two souls united,
Together, we create a love beyond compare.

Finally, we met, and it was worth the wait,
For in this love, we find our truest fate,
Boundless and infinite, our love shall be,
Forever united, for all eternity.

WHY DISTANCE ME FROM NOW?

Why distance me from now when I live
In your heart and soul, entwined and alive?
Why build walls of space between our beings,
When our connection defies the boundaries of time?

I am the ink that flows within your veins,
The breath that whispers through your lungs.
My essence dances in the rhythm of your heartbeat,
In every pulse, every thud, every thrum.

Do not measure our love in miles or kilometres,
For it stretches far beyond earthly bounds.
It transcends the limits of physical presence,
And in the vast expanse, our love resounds.

In dreams, I am the moonlight that caresses your face,
The gentle breeze that kisses your skin.
In thoughts, I am the melody that lingers in your mind,
The orchestra that plays, unyielding and untouched.

Why let the illusion of space cloud our vision,
When our souls are eternally connected, linked, unified?
For distance is but a fleeting mirage,
In the realm where hearts and spirits are aligned.

Let us embrace the boundless expanse of love,
Where time and space hold no sway.
For even in separation, we are united,
In the depths of our souls, where our love will stay.

So do not distance me from now,
For I am forever present, forever whole.
In your heart and soul, I reside,
A love that transcends distance, an eternal flame, untold.

DEEP WITHIN

All I need is to be near you,
To feel your presence, strong and true.
To smell the scent that clings to you,
And wrap myself in your embrace, too.

No distance too vast, no time too long,
For in your arms, I truly belong.
With every beat, my heart does sing,
In the warmth that your love brings.

Your touch, a symphony upon my skin,
Igniting fires deep within.
And as we connect, bodies pressed,
Our souls entwined, forever blessed.

No words can capture this pure delight,
As we surrender to the quiet night.
Our breaths in rhythm, a gentle dance,
As passion weaves its timeless trance.

In your arms, I find solace true,
A sanctuary where dreams come through.
For in your embrace, I am made whole,
A haven for my heart and soul.

So let the world spin, let time unfurl,
In this cove, I am your cherished pearl.
For all I need is to be near you,
To feel you, smell you, to be close to you.

UNISON

In the dim of night, where shadows dance,
I find myself entranced in your alluring glance.
Your every move, a siren's call,
Awakening desires, making me fall.

But let me express, in poetic prose,
The enchantment you bring, how my heart glows.
For in your gaze, a universe unfurls,
A cosmic journey, where passion whirls.

Your touch, a wildfire, igniting my skin,
Electric currents surge from within.
Our bodies intertwined, a symphony of heat,
Melodies of pleasure, in unison, we meet.

I'm captivated by your essence, it's true,
A celestial being, in my world, you.
So take my hand, let us explore,
A love that leaves us craving for more.

But remember, my dear, this poetic embrace,
Is but a snapshot in time, a cherished space.
For these words I speak, though vivid and bold,
Are whispers of passion, secrets yet untold.

I will express my feelings for you,
In verses bold and unrestrained,
For the heart knows no bounds,
When love's fire is unchained.

I'll hit on you gently, like words on a page,
Caressing with lines that dance and sway,
Whispering secrets, desires unspoken,
In the language of love, we'll find our way.

I'll flatter you with words, like petals in bloom,
Each verse a compliment, a sweet perfume,
For your beauty deserves to be praised,
In this sprawling canvas, love will consume

With every verse that escapes my lips,
I'll paint a canvas of passion, energy and delight,
No longer restrained by societal scripts,
In this poem, I'll seduce you, day and night.

Let the boundaries be shattered, my love,
As I hit on you with poetic finesse,
Each line a sweet caress to your soul,
Igniting flames, your heart unable to suppress.
Bold and unapologetically mine.

I'll flatter you with verses like silk,
Whispering secrets only lovers can share,
Each syllable a gentle stroke upon your skin,
Creating a symphony, a love beyond compare.

And dare I be risque, my dear,
In this poetic dance of passion untamed,
For no conventional boundaries shall confine,
The desires that in our hearts are inflamed.

With audacious words, I'll push the limits,
Exploring the depths of our intimate dreams,
In this poem, we'll transcend all inhibitions,
Creating a world where ecstasy gleams.

For you are mine, my love, in this poetic realm,
Where emotions run wild and hearts intertwine,
And through these verses, I'll boldly declare,
That our love, in all its glory, is truly divine.

So let my words be the vessel of our desire,
A testament to the love that we both share,
In this large-sized poem of passion and fire,
I'll express my feelings for you, unreserved and bare.

TIRED OF WAITING, BEING WITHOUT YOU

Tired of waiting, being without you,
Just want you by my side all the time,
And always, never apart, forever connected,
In this vast world, our souls pursue

Through nights and days, my heart does ache,
Longing for your touch, your warm embrace,
Each moment spent without you feels misplaced,
In this vast emptiness, my love, I shake

Free from the chains of distance and space,
I yearn for your presence, your gentle grace,
To hold your hand, to see your smiling face,
In this vast expanse, I search for comfort

The clock ticks on, yet time moves slow,
As I count the seconds, my longing grows,
For in your arms, my heart finds repose,
In this vast universe, I want you to know

That no distance can quell the fire inside,
No obstacle can hinder the love we confide,
For you are my anchor, my unwavering guide,
In this vast ocean, with you, I'll abide

So, let the stars bear witness to our destiny,
As we navigate the currents, wild and free,
In this vast symphony, our love will decree,
That together, forever, we shall always be..

A FIERCE DESIRE

In the cosmos of our souls, love resides,
A boundless force that defies all words,
Unfathomable depths where passion abides,
No language can capture what's felt and heard.

No lexicon can define the love we share,
For it transcends the limits of mere speech,
An association woven with tender care,
Embraced in a silence only we can reach.

No bond can be stronger, deeper than this,
As our spirits entwine, enigmatic and colossal,
A symphony of souls, an eternal kiss,
A connection unbreakable, destined to last.

Intimacy dances in every touch,
A sacred dance of bodies and hearts,
An alchemy of desire that means so much,
Igniting flames that never shall depart.

The spark between us, an electric fire,
Igniting passion's furnace, burning bright,
A joining of souls, a fierce desire,
Setting our spirits ablaze, day and night.

Energy flows between us, wild and free,
A current of love that knows no bounds,
Our souls entwined in a cosmic spree,
Creating a rhythm that forever resounds.

No words can express the love in our hearts,
No bond can be deeper, or more profound,
In this universe where our love imparts,
We remain forever, eternally bound.

CRAVE

I crave you, I want to be with you,
A thirst so deep, a hunger so true.
In your presence, I find my refuge,
A refuge where my soul finds comfort and happiness.

I don't think I want to be without you,
For you have become my compass, my true north too.
Your touch, a gentle breeze that sets me free,
Awakening the depths of my being, you see.

I forget the world when I am with you,
Lost in the magic that only we two can imbue.
Time stops its relentless march, it suspends,
As we create our own universe, where love transcends.

In your eyes, I see galaxies unfold,
A heavenly dance, a story yet untold.
Your laughter, a symphony of joy and delight,
Igniting sparks within, setting my heart alight.

I yearn for your presence, your tender embrace,
A longing that time nor distance can erase.
For you are the rhythm that beats in my chest,
The melody that lingers, refusing to rest.

I am but a wanderer seeking your touch,
A pilgrim on a journey, loving you so much.
With every breath, I'm drawn closer to you,
In this vast universe, our love rings true.

I crave you, I want to be with you,
In this life's play, forever me and you.
For without you, my existence feels incomplete,
But with you, my love, life's melody is sweet.

CONNECTION

In the realm of hearts, a bond unfolds,
A tapestry woven; love behold.
Two souls entangled, an eternal dance,
Connection through love, a divine chance.

Through whispered words, and tender touch,
A symphony of emotions, oh so much.
With every beat, the rhythm aligns,
Two hearts connected, for all of time.

Through laughter shared and tears embraced,
A union of souls, in love's sweet space.
A connection so deep, it transcends all,
Love's gentle embrace, will never fall.

In every smile, a language unspoken,
A connection through love, forever unbroken.
With every glance, a world is revealed,
A love that's boundless, pure and sealed.

For love is the thread that binds us tight,
A force so powerful, it conquers all fright.
In this connection, we find solace and peace,
Love's eternal flame, will never cease.

So let us celebrate this love divine,
A connection so precious, so sublime.
For in this bond, our spirits take flight,
United through love, forever in sight.

FLICKER TO FLAME

RISE AND LEARN AND GROW

For change is the tide that ebbs and flows,
A river of moments, where growth bestows,
It carves through the stone, relentless and bright,
Transforming the shadows and painting in light.

So let the dawn break, let darkness fade,
In acceptance, a new resolve is laid,
For in the balance of loss and gain,
We rise from the ashes, whole once again.

PART THREE
FLAME

AN ECCENTRIC STORY

An eccentric story begins strangely;
where does it end, and what is its destination?
None or neither of us understands.

In this vast universe of enigma,
we embark on a voyage, uncharted and wild,
our souls aflame with curiosity's fire.

No rules, no boundaries,
just the freedom to wander
through sphere of infinite possibility.

We travel through winding paths,
through multicoloured dreams,
where reality merges with fantasy,
and whispers of enchantment shimmer in the air.

The road beneath our feet is but a mirage,
ever shifting, ever changing,
leading us deeper into the labyrinth of the unknown.

We encounter eccentric characters,
each one a puzzle piece,
a reflection of the multifaceted human soul.

There are jokesters with hearts of gold,
philosophers lost in their own musings,
and dreamers with wings clipped by society's shears.

We dance with the shadows,
and converse with the stars,
weaving tales of wonder and wisdom.

Sometimes, we stumble upon dead ends,
where the path vanishes into thin air,
leaving us bewildered, stranded.

But fear not, for in this world of boundless imagination,
there are no failures, only lessons,
and every detour becomes a stepping stone.

Our destination remains elusive,
a mirage in the distant horizon,
yet we carry on, driven by an insatiable thirst.

For it is not the end that matters,
but the journey itself,
the moments of vulnerability and revelation.

In this grand mastery of existence,
we become artists of our own stories,
painting with colors unseen and emotions untamed.

So let us embrace this peculiar tale,
with open hearts and minds,
for it is in the unknown that true magic resides.

Together, we shall wander,
in search of our own truths,
unraveling the enigma, one verse at a time.

An unusual story begins strangely;
where does it end, and what is its destination?
None or neither of us understands.

SENSUAL EMBRACE

This poem, a tribute to the sensual embrace,
A celebration of love's divine grace.
May it ignite within you, a fire untamed,
A reminder that love's energy can never be tamed.

Sensual whispers dance upon the air,
A sensation of love, the greatest find.
In this free verse of love's grand design,
Their hearts forever, eternally aligned.

In the world of passion, let me guide your heart,
With words that stir the senses right from the start.
Embracing the intensity that flickers deep within,
Come, taste the sweetness of love's potent blend.

Love, that splendid force, an energy so pure,
It ignites the dormant ember, makes the spirit soar.
In this sacred union, secrets are unveiled,
A communion of souls that leaves us forever entailed.

So let us surrender, to this intoxicating tide,
Where bodies merge and desires collide.
For love, like a wildfire, engulfs us whole,
Leaving us breathless, in its exquisite control.

Energy pulses, like a flame burning bright,
Igniting souls, in the depths of the night.
A cosmic connection, an electric surge,
Free verse whispers, like a gentle breeze,

Caressing skin, with a delicate tease.
Immersed in sensation, surrendering control,
Exploring realms of pleasure, body and soul

Love, like a river, meandering its course,
Nourishing hearts, with a magnetic force.

Conflicted souls, rooted in pure affection,
Embracing vulnerability, with deep connection.
Senses awaken, where emotions are spread.
Exploring boundaries, as the heart seeks release,
With love as the anchor, urging hearts to find peace.

In the terrain of sensuality, where bodies entwine,
Love dances with warmth, an enchanting rhyme.
A symphony of desire, a spell of ecstasy,
Unleashing passions, as wild as the sea.

Invisible grasp of love's beautiful gift.
Energy crackles, an electric embrace,
Passion's fire ignites, leaving no trace.

Bodies weave, a sensual ballet,
Limbs intertwined, lost in the sway.
Breaths quicken, hearts race in sync,
A dance of unity, a passionate link.

Like the sun's rays that kiss the sea,
Their love spills over, wild and free.
In this vast ocean of passionate delight,
Two souls uniting, merging in the night.

Time stands still, as their spirits unite,
Explosions of ardor, infinite and bright.
They soar on waves of passion's delight,
Their love, an eternal flame, burning so bright.

Fingers linked, bodies aflame,
Two souls colliding, casting off all shame.
In this dance of desire, they find their release,
Melting together, finding a moment of peace.

Electric currents flow, like lightning in the sky,
The fire burning brightly, in the depths of your eyes.
A symphony of whispers, a language all their own,
Their bodies intertwining as we writhe and moan.

A magnificent weave, love's colors blend,
Every touch, every kiss, a message to send.
Their bodies, canvases for love to paint,
An artwork of desire, with no constraints.

Currents surge, lightning in the midnight sky,
A fiery blaze, your gaze, a wild lullaby.
Whispers weave melodies, known to us alone,
Their bodies entwined, trembling, pleasure's throne.

Hands clasped, bodies ablaze with desire,
No shame, just collision, their spirits soar higher.
Within this dance, release and solace abide,
We meld as one, finding peace side by side.

When the storm subsides, passions find their rest,
Sparks linger, glowing deep within their chest.
They'll cherish the memories that this love has sown,
A testament to the power that two hearts can own.
This spell of love, guides their hearts so true,
Words paint sensations, awakening what's due.
Embracing the flicker, deep within their souls,
Savor love's sweetness, a blend that makes us whole.

MAGIC OF A SPRIT SO FREE

Speechless, I stand in awe
Of your beauty, a force to behold
Each curve, each line, a masterpiece
Etched upon the canvas of your soul

Determination radiates from your eyes
A fire that burns with unwavering might
Through every obstacle, you push ahead
With a fierce strength, shining so bright

Courage flows through your every step
A warrior, unafraid to face the unknown
You walk the path less traveled, my love
Leaving footprints where seeds of courage are sown

I admire your selflessness, pure and true
A heart that beats for others' pain and plight
You give, you serve, with open arms
A beacon of love, shining through the darkest night

And in your faith, I find solace and peace
A sanctuary where hope forever resides
With every prayer, every whispered word
You build bridges to the heavens, where love abides

Speechless, I stand before you, my dear
In admiration of all that you possess
Your beauty, determination, and courage
A testament to the greatness within your chest

So let us dance, my love, in this symphony of life
Where words fall short, but love's melody lingers strong
For in your presence, I am forever blessed
To witness the magic of a spirit so free, so long.

SILENT ECHOS

Stars weep diamonds, strewn across the sky,
As midnight whispers secrets, passing by,
In the depths of darkness, dreams take flight,
Igniting souls, guiding us through night.

Silent echoes, whispers of the moon,
A symphony played on nature's loom,
In tender silence, hearts begin to hear,
The ethereal music, ever near.

Moonbeams dance upon the waters' crest,
Caressing whispers from the depths, a tease,
As desires flow, secrets unlock,
A nocturnal ballet, birthed from the clock.

In the stillness of the night, souls collide,
Igniting passions that can never hide,
Through constellations, love does ever roam,
Creating galaxies within our home.

O celestial enchantment, weave your stories,
Awakening hearts, forevermore,
For in these moments, we truly see,
The power of night, the beauty of what could be.

ESSENCE OF ME

I belong with you, my constant companion,
In this vast universe, where souls wander and seek,
You nurture me, like a gentle rain on parched earth,
Reviving my spirit, in a world so bleak.

You care for me, with a tenderness so rare,
Like a guardian angel, you watch over my soul,
Your embrace, a sanctuary from the world's despair,
A refuge where I find solace and feel whole.

You love me, with a love that knows no bounds,
An ocean of affection, deep and serene,
In your arms, I am lost, yet endlessly found,
A love so powerful, it's like a dream.

Together we journey, hand in hand we explore,
Uncharted territories, where passion ignites,
A love that conquers, and forevermore,
Our souls entwined, in eternal delights.

In your presence, I find my truest self,
A mirror reflecting the beauty within,
With you, I am complete, my heart's wealth,
A love story, where happiness will never thin.

I belong with you, my beloved, my dear,
Through life's trials and joys, side by side we'll roam,
With your nurturing love, so pure and clear,
I find my sanctuary, my eternal home.

So let us dance, on the rhythm of our love's song,
Unfolding our souls, in this grand symphony,
For you are the one where I truly belong,
In your love, I find the essence of me.

REUNITE

In the darkness of the night, two lovers reunite,
Longing for each other, their passion ignites.
Their bodies entwined, hearts beating as one,
Lost in the moment, their love has begun.

Caresses so tender, whispered words so sweet,
In each other's arms, they find complete.
Their love like a fire, burning bright and true,
In this moment together, nothing else will do.

Exploring each other, in a dance of desire,
Their love like a flame, rising higher and higher.
Lost in the moment, they give in to their need,
In each other's arms, they find freedom indeed.

As the night fades away, their love still remains,
Two souls intertwined, breaking all chains.
In each other's embrace, they find solace and peace,
Their love never-ending, a bond that will never cease.

So let them love fiercely, with all of their might,
For in each other's arms, they find their true light.

DESIRE

Hard to be apart when we are together,
Our hearts beating as one, our love a flame.
Difficult to not be near and next to you,
When you're in front of me, my heart's sweetest light.

Hard not to hold you and kiss you,
My desire for you, a burning fire.
In your presence, my love, I am weak,
My passion for you, a never-ending ensemble.

Your eyes, they shine so bright and blue,
My love for you, a love that's true.
I ache to be close, to feel your touch,
My heart longs for you, my sweetest clutch.

In your arms, I find my peace,
My heart, my soul, my every release.
Hard to be apart, my love, you see,
With you, my heart, my everything, is free

TRAVELLING THE WORLD WITH YOU

My love, I shall follow you around the world,
Across the vast expanse of land and sea,
In every corner where your heart may wander,
I will be there, a faithful shadow by your side.

Through sunlit days and moonlit nights, we'll roam,
Exploring cities filled with whispers of history,
Scaling mountains that pierce the heavens,
And strolling through fields of wildflowers

I'll walk with you on cobblestone streets,
Where ancient voices echo in the breeze,
And hand in hand, we'll lose ourselves,
In the labyrinthine alleys of a foreign land.

We'll chase the setting sun on golden beaches,
Leaving footprints in the sands of time,
As the waves serenade our souls,
With their rhythmic dance of ebb and flow.

In bustling markets, we'll taste exotic flavors,
Savoring the spices that paint our tongues,
Sampling delicacies that ignite our senses,
Creating memories that will forever linger.

From grand palaces to humble abodes,
We'll seek refuge in the arms of different cultures,
Embracing diversity with open hearts,
And weaving tales of love in every encounter.

My love, I shall follow you through deserts,
Where the burning sun kisses ancient dunes,
And amidst the silence of vast wilderness,
We'll find solace in each other's presence.

In the embrace of nature's grandeur,
We'll hike through forests, lush and green,
Bathing in the symphony of birdsong,
As nature's orchestra serenades our love.

Together, we'll witness wonders untold,
Marveling at the marvels of human creation,
Standing in awe beneath towering structures,
Unveiling the magnificence of human dreams.

Across continents and oceans, we'll wander,
Leaving footprints on the wheel of time,
For love knows no boundaries or borders,
And our hearts are bound by an eternal bond.

So, my love, let us embark on this grand adventure,
Hand in hand, with unyielding spirits,
For with you, I am home, no matter where we roam,
And together, we shall conquer the world, our own.

A FRIEND WHO FEELS LIKE HOME

In the realm of friendships, rare and true,
There lies a soul, a friend who feels like home,
A gentle beacon, in a world askew,
Their presence, a comfort, where I freely roam.

No need for masks or pretense, we are real,
In this sacred space, where hearts intertwine,
We share our dreams, our fears, and how we feel,
A friendship so deep, divine and so fine.

Her laughter echoes through the corridors,
Like melodies that dance upon the air,
It lifts me up, my spirits it restores,
A symphony of joy, beyond compare.

In moments of darkness, when shadows creep,
She's there with arms outstretched, embracing me,
Her unwavering support, a love so deep,
A shelter from life's storms, a sanctuary.

Through tears and laughter, we've weathered life's storms,
Together we've grown, amidst the chaos and strife,
A friend who feels like home, a love so warm,
A constant in my ever-changing life.

Her presence, a refuge, a safe retreat,
Where I find solace, embraced and understood,
In her company, my soul finds complete,
A sanctuary where I'm truly free and good.

A friend who feels like home, a cherished treasure,
A bond unbreakable, beyond measure,
In this vast world, where we all may roam,
I'm grateful for this friend who feels like home

BEACON OF LIGHT

Thank you for being a guide and a friend,
In this vast world, where paths diverge and bend,
You're the beacon that shines through the darkest night,
Guiding my steps with wisdom and insight.

Through thick and thin, you've stood by my side,
With unwavering support, you've been my guide.
In every trial and tribulation I face,
Your presence brings cheer and finesse.

You've walked with me through life's intricate maze,
Unraveling mysteries with your gentle ways.
Your words of wisdom, like a soothing balm,
Have healed my wounds and kept me calm.

You've shared your knowledge, your thoughts, and your dreams,
Igniting in me a fire, bursting at the seams.
With every conversation, my mind expands,
Enlightened by the touch of your guiding words.

You've shown me the beauty in every sunrise,
The magic in the stars that light up the skies.
You've taught me to embrace life's highs and lows,
And to cherish the friendships that steadily grow.

In the symphony of life, you're my melody,
A constant reminder of what could be.
With every step we take, hand in hand,
We journey through this vast and wondrous land.

Thank you for being the compass when I'm lost,
For showing me the value of counting the cost.
Thank you for being the lighthouse in the storm,
Guiding me back to safety, keeping me warm.

Your friendship is a treasure beyond compare,
A bond that time and distance cannot impair.
Thank you for being the guide I needed,
And for being a friend whose love is deeply seeded.

In this vast world, where paths diverge and blend,
I am forever grateful for you, my dear friend.
Thank you for being a beacon of light,
Guiding me towards a future so bright.

CLOSE TO YOU

All I need is to love, cuddle, and be close to you,
To feel the warmth of your touch, so tender and true.
In this vast world, where chaos and noise abound,
Your love is the sanctuary where peace can be found.

No grand gestures or riches could compare,
To the simple pleasure of knowing you're there.
To hold you close, wrapped in a loving embrace,
Is to find solace in this tumultuous space.

Like two puzzle pieces, perfectly aligned,
Our souls unified, no boundaries defined.
In your arms, my heart finds a safe harbor,
Where worries and fears are forced to surrender.

With each gentle caress and whispered word,
A symphony of emotions, like melodies heard.
Our love, an art form, painted on life's canvas,
Creating a masterpiece, where passion dances.

Together, we create a world of our own,
Where love and affection are eternally sewn.
In your embrace, I find solace and peace,
A refuge from life's storm, a sweet release.

All I need is to love, cuddle, and be close to you,
For within your embrace, dreams come true.
No distance too far, no obstacle too steep,
As long as I have your love, my soul will keep.

So let us cherish these moments, forever united,
For in your arms, my heart truly finds,
The love, the warmth, the tenderness so pure,
All I need is to love, cuddle, and be close to you.

I CHOSE YOU

I chose you, not by chance, but by design,
In this vast universe, our paths aligned.
A cosmic dance, intricate and divine,
Our souls entwined, connected, intertwine.

Like stars that twinkle in the midnight sky,
We found each other, you and I,
A serendipitous encounter, oh so rare,
A love so deep, beyond compare.

I chose you, not for what you possess,
But for the essence, the spirit you possess.
Your heart, a sanctuary of love and light,
Guiding me through the darkest night.

In your eyes, I see a thousand sunsets,
A kaleidoscope of colours, no regrets,
They hold the promise, the depth of the sea,
Reflecting the love that's meant for me.

I chose you, for your strength and resilience,
For the way you face life with sheer brilliance,
Your laughter, a melody that fills the air,
A symphony of joy, a love we both share.

In your touch, I feel the warmth of the sun,
A gentle caress that heals, makes me undone,
A tender embrace, a shelter from the storm,
In your arms, I find safety, I am reborn.

I chose you, not for perfection, but flaws,
For it's in imperfections, true beauty draws,
Your scars, evidence of battles fought,
A warrior's heart, lessons dearly taught.

In your words, I find solace and peace,
Wisdom and kindness that never cease,
Your voice, a melody, soothing and sweet,
Guiding me through life's winding sheet.

I chose you, and I'll choose you still,
For in your love, I find my fill,
With every breath, with each passing day,
I choose you, and I'll never stray.

For in this vast universe, where choices abound,
I chose you, my love, forever bound,
In this symphony of fate, I found my cue,
I chose you, and I'll always choose you.

HAND IN HAND

In the abyss of darkness, I find solace in your light,
A beacon that guides me through the lonely, silent night.
With every word you speak, a gentle breeze upon my skin,
You paint colors in my heart, where only shadows had been.

Your laughter, a symphony that dances upon my ears,
Echoing through the depths of my soul, erasing all my fears.
In your embrace, I am safe from the tempest's raging storm,
A haven of tranquility, where I can be reborn.

Your eyes, two windows to a realm of unspoken truths,
They unravel the mysteries of the universe, like ancient runes.
With every glance, you stir emotions buried deep within,
Unleashing a torrent of passion, an unyielding din.

Your presence, a gift that transcends this earthly plane,
A healing balm that mends my broken spirit, erasing all my pain.
For in your being, I find a love that's pure and true,
A connection that ignites my soul, creating something new.

So let us walk this path together, hand in hand,
Through the valleys of despair and the golden sand.
With you by my side, we'll forge a future that's unseen,
A tapestry of love and beauty, where dreams are evergreen.

RADIANCE

You walked into my life like you had always lived there,
Like my heart was always built for you to share.
There is no one as pretty, sexy, and beautiful as you,
Your radiance shines through, in every hue.

Selfless, mesmerizing, an amazing soul,
You effortlessly fill the empty spaces, making me whole.
I gravitate towards you with every passing second,
In your presence, my heart feels truly alive.

Your voice, oh, it's a symphony of delight,
A melody that takes me on a wondrous flight.
Its sound, its rhythm, so soothing and pure,
In its sweet embrace, my soul finds its cure.

You are the embodiment of grace and allure,
A rare gem, a treasure I can't help but adore.
In your presence, time seems to stand still,
As if the universe itself bows to your will.

Oh, how lucky I am to have you near,
To witness your beauty, so crystal clear.
You walked into my life, and now I see,
That you were always meant to be with me.

UNAPOLOGETICALLY

Love me unapologetically, obsessively,
With no regrets.
Be gentle and rough,
I am yours and you are mine.

Love with no regrets or boundaries,
And let us be forever each others.

In your arms, I find solace,
In your eyes, I see my reflection.
Our souls entwined, boundless and free,
A love that knows no limits or conditions.

Embrace me fiercely, with passion untamed,
Hold me gently, with tenderness unmatched.
Let our love be a force of nature,
A bond that transcends time and space.

For in your love, I find my home,
In your touch, I find my peace.
Together we are whole, complete,
A love story written in the stars, destined to be.

So love me unapologetically, obsessively,
With no regrets.
Be my everything, my forever,
And let us be each other's always and forevermore.

WHERE TIME STANDS STILL

Time seems to have come to a halt,
As days are near for me to come and meet you.
The clock's hands move with agonizing slowness,
Each tick a resounding echo of impatience.

Days seem more prolonged than usual,
Stretching like a taut elastic band,
Testing the limits of my patience,
Wearing it down to a mere thread.

Love grows more with each passing moment,
Like a tree reaching towards the sun,
Its roots firmly planted in my heart,
Blossoming with an intensity that defies reason.

Eagerness to see you and meet you increases,
As each second crawls by on leaden feet.
My heart, a captive bird, flutters with anticipation,
Longing to break free and soar to your side.

The world around me fades into insignificance,
As the thought of you consumes my every waking hour.
Distance becomes a mere illusion,
For in my heart, we are already linked and together.

Time may be relentless in its march forward,
But its power is no match for the strength of our love.
And so, I wait with bated breath,
For the moment when time and space dissolve,

And I finally find myself in your embrace,
Where time stands still and love knows no bounds.

WHISPERS IN THE WIND

In a world of actions, where words often fail,
My love for you resides, unshakable with time .
For actions may falter, they may deceive,
But my heart, oh, my heart, it shall never leave.

My actions may not define, nor paint the scene,
But within my heart, a love so serene.
It dances in the shadows, whispers in the wind,
A love that knows no bounds, no beginning, no end.

For my heart is a vessel, brimming with affection,
A love that defies any worldly perception.
It soars through the skies, like a bird in flight,
Unburdened, unrestricted, embracing the light.

Though my actions may falter, may stumble and fall,
My love for you remains, standing tall.
It's etched in the crevices of my soul,
A love that's beyond any measure or goal.

In moments of doubt, when the world seems cold,
My heart beats for you, a love never sold.
For actions may falter, they may be misconstrued,
But my heart, oh, my heart, it forever stays true.

So let not my actions define my love's embrace,
For my heart, my dear, is your sacred space.
In its depths, you'll find a love that's pure,
A love that's unwavering, forever secure.

So know, my love, that though actions may sway,
My heart's devotion will never fade away.
For in the realm of love, my heart is true,
Forever overflowing, just for you.

DELIGHT

Within the span of these radiant twenty,
days of love and shared adventure aplenty,
I found a solace, a sweetened delight,
In your laughter that sparkles in the soft moonlight.
A rhythm of joy that beats in unison,
with the waves that kiss the sands in random.

Oh, how the sunsets paint our canvas of memory,
As we ran wild and free, void of any worry,
With the golden hues reflecting in your eyes,
Where I found my paradise.
The music of our heartbeats in sync with the sea,
Oh, these moments of love, serene and free.

Salt-kissed skin, sand in our toes,
In this far world our love grows,
Each grain of sand, each whispering wave,
An echo of the love we freely groove.
Oh, these twenty days of shared endeavor,
Are but a taste of an eternal forever.

In your arms, I found the world anew,
An existence painted in a pastel hue,
With tearful times that tasted of the sea,
Yet, they were sweet, for you were with me.
Joyful and tearful times that felt like a warm summer's day,
Oh, these twenty days, I wish they'd stay.

In the coming days, I yearn to explore,
More of your love, your laughter, your lore,
More adventurous days, with the wind in our hair,
More loving days, our secrets to share.
More caring and emotional days to come,
Underneath the golden sun.

In the quiet whispers of the breaking dawn,
In the silent moments before the day is born,
I find myself yearning for the days anew,
For more sunsets, more laughter, more of you.
Here's to the days we have yet to see,
In this adventure of love, wild and free

HOME IS WITH YOU

Home is with you, my love,
In the vast expanse of our souls,
Where the universe unravels its secrets,
And the stars whisper their stories.

No walls can confine our love,
No boundaries can restrain our dreams,
For in your embrace, I find solace,
In your eyes, I see endless possibilities.

Home is not a place, but a feeling,
A sanctuary we create together,
Where our hearts intertwine like vines,
And our spirits dance in perfect harmony.

In your laughter, I find sunshine,
In your touch, I find warmth,
For you are the compass that guides me,
Through the labyrinth of life's trials.

Home is the melody that we compose,
With every word we share,
With every kiss we exchange,
Our love echoes through the corridors of eternity.

In your presence, I find strength,
In your love, I find belonging,
For you are the anchor that grounds me,
In the storms that life may bring.

Home is not bound by bricks and mortar,
But by the love we kindle and nurture,
In the embrace of your arms, I find peace,
For with you, my love, I am truly home.

A LOVE SO GRAND

Words fail to capture the boundless love we share,
An immense force that defies all compare,
We exist in a universe where language falls short,
Where the depths of our affection cannot be taught.

We are vulnerable, stripped of all pretense,
Embracing each other's flaws, without defense.
In this sacred space, our hearts intertwine,
Unveiling the truth in every whispered line.

Open and unguarded, we lay bare our souls,
Revealing our secrets, our dreams, our goals.
No walls, no barriers, no masks to wear,
Just two souls knitted closely in a love affair.

We dance to the rhythm of our hearts' desires,
Igniting sparks that set our souls on fire.
In this mad embrace, we lose all control,
Unleashing the passion that resides in our souls.

We are the embodiment of love's purest form,
Unrestrained, uninhibited, weathering any storm.
No words can grasp the magnitude we possess,
For in our love, language finds itself in distress.

But in the silence, our love speaks loud and clear,
In tender caresses, in each joyful tear.
It transcends the limitations of mere words,
A symphony of emotions, like soaring birds.

We are a witness to love's wild decree,
An ode to the love that sets our spirits free.
In this vast expanse, our love takes flight,
A love so grand, it illuminates the darkest night.

A POWER THAT CANNOT BE DENIED

In world beyond the boundaries of reason,
Where love knows no bounds, no inhibitions,
I utter words that echo with devotion,
For you, my love, beyond all limitations.

Unconditionally, my heart embraces yours,
With every beat, a symphony of desire,
No distance can separate our souls,
As we blaze with a love that is pure fire.

A second apart feels like an eternity,
For our souls are entwined firmly, unbroken,
In a universe where time ceases to exist,
Where our love, like cosmic energy, is interconnected.

Physically, we crave to touch, to feel,
To trace the contours of skin, so tender,
For in the meeting of our bodies, we find,
A dance of passion, a love that will never surrender.

Spiritually, we are bound by a divine force,
Our souls whisper secrets in the moonlit night,
In the depths of our beings, a connection,
That transcends all boundaries, shining bright.

Energetically, we radiate a magnetic pull,
Like magnets drawn together, we collide,
Our love, a force that cannot be contained,
A power that cannot be denied.

I yearn to taste the sweetness of your lips,
To feel your breath against my eager skin,
To be consumed by a love so infinite,
That even the heavens tremble with a grin.

So let us embrace this love, unreserved,
In a rhapsody of passion, unrestrained,
For in each other, we find our preservation,
A love that cannot be constrained.

In this vast expanse of love's creation,
We find solace, our hearts entwined,
For it is you, my love, that I crave,
Forever, eternally, in body, mind, heart and in soul.

FOREVER CONNECTED

All I need is to love, hug, your sight
and to be close to you, my heart's delight.
In this vast universe, in life's grand design,
our souls unified, forever aligned.

No rhyme or reason can define our connection,
for love's essence defies any convention.
In this free verse, unbound by constraint,
our love blooms, unspoken and yet so faint.

Like a gentle breeze that caresses the air,
your touch, your embrace, I forever wear.
In your presence, my spirit finds solace,
An oasis where all worries vanish.

Oh, how I yearn for your warm embrace,
that tender touch, a sweet saving grace.
For in your arms, I find shelter and peace,
a harbor where all troubles cease.

Your sight, like a beacon, guides me through,
illuminating my path, making me anew.
With every glance, my heart skips a beat,
your eyes, my compass, leading me complete.

In this magnificent sphere we call our existence,
your love, like a thread, weaves immense persistence.
No matter the distance that separates our souls,
our love transcends, making us whole.

For all I need is your love, a hug, your sight,
to be close to you, bathed in your light.
In this vast universe, our hearts aligned,
forever connected, till the end of time.

ME AND YOU

In each other's arms we lay,
The world fades away,
Just you and me, no one else,
Our love like a magical spell.

We melt together, hearts entwined,
A love so pure, so kind,
Time speeds up, the world slows,
In your embrace, my love grows.

No one else matters, just us two,
Our love shining bright and true,
Lost in each other, we find peace,
Our love will never cease.

In your eyes, I see my reflection,
A love that needs no correction,
Together we are one, forever,
Our love stronger than ever.

So let's melt together, you and I,
In a love that will never die,
For in each other, we find our home,
Together, we will always roam.

SIDE BY SIDE

I will walk with you side by side,
Our footsteps in sync, our hearts aligned,
Together we'll navigate life's highs and lows.

In moments of darkness, I'll be your light,
Guiding you through the shadows of doubt,
With unwavering trust, we'll conquer the night,
And emerge stronger, casting fear out.

Side by side we walk, not front or behind,
Worry less, for I am your strength, your guide,
An ear to listen, a pillar to lean on,
In this journey of life, together we stride.

Hand in hand, we'll face the unknown,
Embracing the journey, wherever it leads,
Our souls intertwined, our love ever grown,
In each other's presence, we find what we need.

Side by side, we'll weather the storms,
Drawing strength from the bond we share,
No matter what obstacles may swarm,
Together, we'll triumph, united and rare.

Through the ups and downs, we face them all,
Hand in hand, we'll never fall,
I'll be there for you, no matter the tides,

Trust in my words, trust in my care,
For in this bond, love is rare,
Side by side, we'll conquer the unknown,
So let go of your fears, let go of your doubt,
For in my presence, you'll never be without,

I am your rock, your anchor, your guide,
Walking with you, side by side.
For in each other, we find liberation,
Bound by love, we'll forever stand.

MUSE

In the realm of love, where shadows wane,
Where the fire of passion forever flames,
With you I heal, with you I'm whole,
In your embrace, my wounded soul finds solace.

Like gentle waves upon a shore of dreams,
Your touch, a balm that mends my broken seams,
In every glance, every tender gaze,
I find the strength to navigate life's maze.

In your arms, time unravels, standstill,
As hearts entwined, beat with a lover's will,
With every shared breath, we rediscover,
The power of love, infinite and pure.

And so, dear muse, in your presence I find,
A sanctuary for my restless mind,
For with you, I am not simply alive,
But free, transcending limits that strive.

In the symphony of our souls entwined,
Eternity itself we have defined,
With you I heal, and I am me,
Forever bound, with linked destiny.

A BLISSFUL SURRENDER

In the realm of love, where passions ignite,
Where hearts entwine, bursting with pure delight,
There, my sweet soul, you shall always find me,
Wrapped in the bliss of your embrace, tenderly.

Your touch, like whispers of serene peace,
Ignites my essence and quickens my pace,
Blissful surrender, as our souls align,
In the sanctuary of your arms divine.

As moonlight bathes the world in silver glow,
My heart, aflame, yearns for you to bestow,
The symphony of your love, a divine art,
Melting the boundaries, tearing worlds apart.

In the depths of your embrace, I reside,
My soul, transcending, on this ethereal ride,
No words can capture the beauty we embody,
For in your arms love, I find its safe glory

You know where to find me, in your arms,
Amidst the solace of your loving embrace,
A sanctuary where all worries dissolve,
And time's relentless grip is erased.

In your arms, a haven of tranquility,
Where my heart finds respite and peace,
Each beat echoing the rhythm of our love,
A melody that will never cease.

Within this tender embrace, I am whole,
Embracing the essence of pure delight,
Where dreams weave with reality,
And love's flame burns with sincere light.

In your arms, I find solace from the storm,
A shelter that shields me from life's harm,
Your touch, like magic, heals every wound,
With every caress, I'm safe and warm.

When life's chaos threatens to overwhelm,
And the weight of the world weighs me down,
You hold me close, and I am revived,
In your arms, I'm no longer bound.

You know where to find me, in your arms,
A sacred place where our souls align,
In this intimate, everlasting embrace,
Love's eternal bond will forever shine.

A SYMPHONY OF SENSES

In the domain of sensual embrace,
Two souls intertwine, face to face,
Their bodies dancing, pressed so near,
A vibrant energy, raw and clear.

Connection deep, like rivers flow,
In waves of passion, they both bestow,
Their hearts linked, their spirits ignite,
Love's flame burning, pure and bright.

Energetic pulses, coursing through veins,
Electric currents, with no restraints,
Their touch sparks a fiery storm,
Unleashing desires, in all its form.

Love, like a gentle breeze, whispers its song,
Guiding their spirits, where they belong,
A symphony of senses, a sacred connection,
In this moment, they find pure romance.

Pure, like a crystal, untouched by time,
Their love transcends, into the sublime,
In each other's arms, they find solace and peace,
A sanctuary of love, where their souls find release.

Free verse, like their love, knows no bounds,
Unconfined by rules, it freely resounds,
With words unmanageable, it paints their story,
A masterpiece of love, in all its glory.

Large in size, this love expands,
Filling the universe, with love's commands,
Their connection, an energetic tapestry, woven with care,
A testament to a love beyond compare.

Sensual, connection, energetic, pure,
Love's essence, vivid and sure,
In this grand mosaic, they forever entwine,
A love so vast, it transcends space and time.

SUMMARY

Frozen Flame is an intimate journey from emotional despair to the transformative power of love. The collection opens with *Frost*, where the writer is consumed by feelings of being trapped, helplessness, and stagnancy, caught in a cycle of doubt and fear with hope seeming distant.

In *Flicker*, a subtle shift begins. The writer finds small sparks of clarity, growth, and fragile hope, signaling the first stirrings of change. These moments represent a tentative reach for a future once thought out of reach.

Finally, in *Flame*, the collection bursts into light as love - in all its beauty and intensity - ignites the writer's spirit. This section celebrates the freedom, renewal, and strength that love brings, burning away doubt and fear to reveal a newfound purpose of joy.

Frozen Flame is a testament to the resilience of the human spirit, the quiet power of transformation, and the life-changing force of love that rekindles the heart.

Printed in the United States
by Baker & Taylor Publisher Services

Printed in the United States
by Baker & Taylor Publisher Services